QUAKER QUI[CKS]

Money and Soul:
Quaker Faith and Practice and the Economy

Quaker Quicks is a new series from Christian Alternative focusing upon aspects of Quaker faith and theology. Beginning with *Quaker Roots and Branches* the series will build into a valuable resource both for Quakers and those interested in this unique expression of belief, practice and theology. Watch out for upcoming titles on Quaker theology, faith and practice, and studies in social aspects such as economics and pacifism.

Current other titles...
Quaker Roots and Branches - John Lampen
Telling the Truth about God - Rhiannon Grant
What Do Quakers Believe? - Geoffrey Durham

QUAKER QUICKS

Money and Soul:
Quaker Faith and Practice
and the Economy

Pamela Haines

CHRISTIAN
ALTERNATIVE

Winchester, UK
Washington, USA

JOHN HUNT PUBLISHING

First published by Christian Alternative Books, 2018
Christian Alternative Books is an imprint of John Hunt Publishing Ltd.,
No. 3 East St., Alresford, Hampshire SO24 9EE, UK
office@jhpbooks.net
www.johnhuntpublishing.com
www.christian-alternative.com

For distributor details and how to order please visit the 'Ordering' section on our website.

Text copyright: Pamela Haines 2017
Cover photo: Quaker Climate Justice protest at the British Museum

ISBN: 978 1 78904 089 0
978 1 78904 090 6 (ebook)
Library of Congress Control Number: 2018948897

A CIP catalogue record for this book is available from the British Library.

Design: Stuart Davies

UK: Printed and bound by CPI Group (UK) Ltd, Croydon, CR0 4YY
US: Printed and bound by Thomson-Shore, 7300 West Joy Road, Dexter, MI 48130

We operate a distinctive and ethical publishing philosophy in all areas of our business, from our global network of authors to production and worldwide distribution.

Contents

Preface 1

Foreword 3

Introduction 5

1: Integrity 13

2: Equality 21

3: Simplicity 29

4: Stewardship/Regeneration 37

5: Peace 45

6: Community 53

Conclusion 61

Generals and politicians claim to be the experts on peace and security, advising us to leave the matter in their capable hands. Quakers, leaning on our long-standing Peace Testimony, have boldly said "No! Their expertise is based in flawed assumptions, and can never get us to peace. Even though we've never known a world without war, we hold fast to our deepest beliefs, and say that killing people is wrong." We are confident, outspoken, tenacious, passionate and engaged.

When it comes to economics, however, we bow down to the experts and say, "Okay. It all seems really complicated and you sound confident, so we cede that whole territory to you." Yet what if their expertise is based on flawed assumptions that can never get the world to prosperity? Even though we've never known an economic system that works for everybody, what if we could hold to our deepest beliefs—that greed is not the source of well-being, and integrity is more important than growth? What if we could be equally confident, outspoken, tenacious, passionate, and engaged?

Preface

I write to blow on coals. I see it as sacred work, trying to gather my experience and insight and understanding of truth, as in a bellows, and send it out, hoping that it might find coals that are just waiting for this gust of air to spark into flame.

There are so many ways to fall short in that goal. Have I used myself well as bait, showing not just my conclusions, but my stumbling efforts to arrive at them? Have I been a good sculptor, taking the rough block of thinking, and carving away all the excess to reveal its intended shape? Have I translated adequately, letting the dense thinking of others (often economists in this case) work in me and become mine, so it comes back out in language that is accessible and a context that invites people in? Have I told a story that others can intuitively recognize as their own, one that starts on common territory then leads on, past where they may have traveled before? Have I offered both solid ground on which to stand and a nudge off of stuck places? Have I given people heart to stretch and imagine something new?

If I can do all this, if I can write in that light and power that allows my words to speak to the condition of others and be a blessing to them, then I truly feel that I have received a blessing in return.

* * *

This book has been simmering for a long time. My father opened the door for me on economics as a child, a gift that I treasure more and more. I am grateful to other Quaker economic thinkers for helping to light the way, especially John Woolman in the eighteenth century and Kenneth Boulding in the twentieth. I have been supported by members of our Friends Economic Integrity Project in Philadelphia, and by Quakers in the southwestern

1

US who took a chance and invited me to speak at their yearly gathering on the topic of money, integrity and community. My friend George Lakey has offered invaluable encouragement in the leap into the publishing world, and I have been sustained in all by my partner, Chuck Esser.

* * *

All the quotes that begin the chapters are taken from *Quaker Faith and Practice: The book of Christian discipline of the Yearly Meeting of the Religious Society of Friends (Quakers) in Britain.*

Foreword

George Lakey
Author, *Viking Economics: How the Scandinavians got it right and how we can, too*

Both economics and ethics seem to attract complicated and abstract prose, but this is a book that reads like a relaxed fireside conversation with a thoughtful friend.

Although Pamela Haines was reared by an economist father and has done her share of graduate work, here she shares decades of clarifying questioning. Who are we, anyway, in our daily lives and work and relationships? What matters most? And, in my favorite phrase of hers, when it comes to the economy, "what rings true?"

She generously shares her personal story in this account of Quakers' relating to economic questions. She also invites us, the readers, to look to our own experience for guidance. In each chapter she probes the implications not only in our personal lives but also in the wider community.

Her placing economic issues in the context of what we now understand about ecology comes not from a wish to be trendy but from decades of careful observation. I especially appreciate her refreshing approach to that central question: "Is economic growth a good thing?"

She doesn't flinch when she looks at the challenges we face these days. As a reader I felt respected, and also am aware of her sense of history. After all, in both the United Kingdom and the United States the Great Depression was a period of bleak news and grim forebodings, then to be followed by the suffering of wartime. Out of that period grew new vitality and fresh vision for change, and a determination to reverse the downward spiral by making some major changes in economic institutions.

3

Hard times give rise to competing narratives. During the Depression Aldous Huxley published *Brave New World*, and we have no lack of dystopian presentations in our media today. Pamela Haines is quite willing to stare bad news in the face, but she protects us from "overwhelm" by anchoring her story in the old wisdom of Quaker testimonies which themselves line up with ancient scriptural sources.

This knack for acknowledging the bad news while acting for a better tomorrow is not by any means confined to Quakers. Martin Luther King, Jr., led campaigns in cities where "peaceful race relations" prevailed and, before long, encountered eruptions of racist hate, bombings, police dogs, and the like. At the time some criticized the Nobel Peace Prize committee for giving the award to such a disturber of the peace. King said in his defense that the violence of race and class was already there, under the surface, and that nonviolent campaigns serve the larger good by exposing truths too long denied.

Seventeenth-century Quakers often called themselves Friends of Truth, and they were trouble-makers as well. There's less need to make trouble when Falseness is no longer hegemonic.

I see Pamela Haines in that tradition, daring to unmask the truth about economic structures even though we might be trying to avoid it. She follows the old advice: "Afflict the comfortable, and comfort the afflicted."

Those readers who happen not to like conflict have all the more reason to take this little book to heart and move earlier, rather than later, to mend a broken economic system. Waiting for the suffering on the margins to become general is, indeed, waiting for trouble. Happily, the chapters do not stop at noting the fractures, but go on to suggest ways to mend.

Introduction

You will say, "Christ saith this, and the apostles say this"; but what canst thou say?
Margaret Fell, 1694

The economy, as we usually encounter it, has nothing to do with values or faith. The market caters to no religious belief, nor does the "invisible hand." It is all a matter of science, we are assured: economists have mastered the mathematical formulas for growth and prosperity. Our role as individuals is simply to work, consume and save, each adding our bit to the sum totals of economic activity that will keep the system humming along; the experts will take care of everything else.

This breezy values-free story, however, has never been a good fit with the religion I was raised in. Economic issues seem to crop up in Quaker faith and practice at every turn. A search for answers to questions around faith and economics has been central to my journey, and I have tasted the power of applying faith values to our economic story.

Absorbing Quaker values

I was born into Quakerism, but just barely. My parents had been part of a small group that were new to Quakerism and eager to start a new meeting. I was the first child in my family born to our meeting. We didn't have our own place of worship, and I have just two memories from the first place we met. It wasn't long after the end of the Korean War, and we had taken on a project of contributing to housing reconstruction there. A gifted older child had made a model of a Korean house, and with every small increment of money raised, we added a tile to the model. I felt involved and connected — part of something meaningful that was growing before my eyes. We always sang before the beginning of meeting for worship, and one time we children were told that they were making a new hymnal and wanted suggestions about which songs to include. It was amazing to discover that we were part of something larger, and that those people out there, whoever they were, cared about what the little children in our meeting thought.

When I was five or six years old, our meeting began renting in a new place, a big old house that had seen better times, the national headquarters of a peace organization. There was a spacious room with big windows where we met for meeting for worship. The children stayed in meeting for the first fifteen minutes, then went off for Sunday School in one of the other rooms—there were so many! In a Sunday School project one year, we drew while my mother read stories to us from different parts of the world. Then we made a book from enormous sheets of thick cardboard, each page a collage of our creations from one country. I remember learning about Japanese haiku and Pacific Island bark cloth, and seeing our growing picture of the world come together in that big beautiful book.

It was harder to know what to do in those first fifteen minutes in meeting. I had learned the concept—we were listening for God's word, and if somebody was moved to speak they would stand and share a message. But what exactly should we be doing? I remember looking at faces, counting tiles, being bored, but not unpleasantly so. One Sunday as I looked out the window at the brown of winter, I started noticing that it wasn't just one color. There were different shades of brown, and the more closely I looked, the more diversity and beauty I saw. And then—this is the thing I will never forget—someone stood up to give a message. He spoke about the colors of winter, and how there is beauty to be found there if we just pay attention. It was a revelation. Something was happening in this room. I was not alone. We were connected in spirit.

When I was a teenager, our meeting finally moved to its own

home, a very modest pre-fab building on land that had been donated by one of our members. I remember the planning of the space, the pride of ownership, the big meeting room with the long benches and central fireplace. At Christmas time we put a tree in the open space in the middle, and people were invited during worship to bring something they valued as a gift to the tree. An elderly man with respiratory problems stood up one year and blew into a little plastic bag. "I bring the gift of breath," he said. As he fastened the bag to a branch of the tree, I felt moved and filled.

Decades later, I participated in an exercise where we were asked to think of a safe place from our childhood. I thought of the rooms in our house, the lawn, the garden, the woods, but none of them struck a chord. Then I thought of the meetinghouse. That was it. That was where I felt safe. My parents loved us all but the tension in our house was often thick, and their unspoken unmet adult needs vibrated. I felt confused and burdened by conflicts I couldn't understand or solve. At meeting the love came through without conditions. My spirit was nourished. I knew the grown-ups were committed to listening for and responding to truth as well as they were able, and I rested in that knowledge.

The two basic tenets of our Quaker faith that I was taught rang true to me. First there is that of God in everyone. Therefore, we are called to listen for that of God in ourselves and reach for that of God in others. Second, revelation of truth did not end with the Buddha or Moses or Jesus or Mohammed. We are called to be open to—and alert for—the continuing revelation of truth in our lives. As individual insights are tested with the wisdom of our forebears and the shared experience of our faith community, we can grow in our understanding of truth.

Living out Quaker values

But how could I tell that I was a Quaker as I led my life? Since we were first generation, we had no family lore or traditions to lean on. The only guiding framework we had was what Quakers called the "testimonies": simplicity, peace, integrity, community, equality and stewardship. Looking back, I can see how they shaped my family's approach to life.

Simplicity and peace were the only ones we talked about at all, and simplicity came first. We strived as a family to live simply. We grew most of our vegetables in a big garden, sewed most of our clothes, tented on vacation. We rarely went to the movies, never stayed in a hotel or motel, and I can remember only one time when we all ate out. We never shopped for pleasure. The Christmas presents we gave and received were mostly homemade. When I was eleven, and the sixth child was a baby, we built an addition to our house, and everyone had a job.

Other families in the rapidly growing suburbs of New York City where I grew up made different choices, but we stood by ours with pride. I remember the pressure in high school to seek acceptance and popularity in the clothes you wore, and how I made a conscious decision to not play that game. I was a Quaker, and we understood the value of simplicity.

The only time we used the word "testimony" was in relation to peace. The Quaker Peace Testimony was central in shaping our sense of who we were as a people; it almost had the power of a creedal belief. My father had been a conscientious objector in World War II, as were many Quaker men, but how we were supposed to live out the testimony as children was not very clear.

Opportunity came during the Cold War era air-raid drills in high school. Because of our Peace Testimony we were officially exempt from participation in these drills, so the one or two of us in class would quietly leave for the principal's office till they were over. With my religious identity so visible to my peers, I felt a mixture of pride and discomfort. I was standing up, but had I really made an independent decision about what I believed, or was I just going along with an alternative that came pre-packaged and without cost?

Defining peace more broadly, the models I got at home had significant limitations. My parents never raised their voices, never hit out in anger, but it was clear that conflict roiled below the surface. The extreme conflict avoidance that I experienced was like the family version of peace at any price, and it did not serve us well.

The testimony on integrity was a sleeper in our house. I would say that my parents had a pretty decent baseline of integrity. They didn't lie, cheat or steal. But it was in my meeting community that I witnessed stands of conscience. When I was thirteen, my Sunday School teacher went on a fast in protest of the Vietnam War, and came close to death. I remember a social studies class at school during that time when the teacher said something about how no sensible person would oppose the war. I raised my hand (in fear and trembling—I was not an outspoken child) and spoke up for those who, in conscience, could not agree. It was a moment when I wanted more than anything to remain silent, but knew I could not.

The testimony on equality is a precious one to Quakers. Early Friends refused to take their hats off to their "betters." Men and women were always assumed to be equally able to preach. Slavery was condemned as an abominable affront. Though many Quakers fell far short in living out these values over the years, they could be called out on the inconsistency of their practice.

Reflecting on my childhood, I particularly value how we girls were treated equally. Competence was prized over femininity, and we were proud to drive tractors and do construction. My parents' decision to live in an interracial and interreligious community—a rarity in that early post-war era—was an expression of their commitment to equality as well. On the other hand, their personal relationship was mired in male dominance and traditional gender role expectations, and their understanding of social equality did not extend to class. Yet my training was strong enough that I came of age with a deep desire to overcome the barriers that separated me from any other human being.

I was immersed in community as a child—in my Quaker meeting and in the community where I grew up. As we shared our lives with others in a variety of ways I gained a strong understanding of the value of community, and it was a blessing to be known by many adults outside our family. I remember the little old lady who stood at the door of our meetinghouse and greeted every child by name. We always received a birthday card from her, on behalf of the meeting, and each time I felt a rush of delighted surprise that she knew our birthdays and cared enough to reach out.

Yet there was a way, in the midst of all this community, that we kept to ourselves and were not known. My parents did not ask for help with their relationship, and I did not share my struggles. When our Sunday School teacher told us, the year I was thirteen, that we could choose what we wanted to talk about, I remember the shock that somebody wanted to know what was going on inside me, and my hesitant wish to show myself.

Stewardship, in its most common form in Quaker practice, relates to care of possessions, and I picture old men making conservative decisions about management of property and investments. At home the testimony had a little more life. We valued what we had, learned the skills of mending and repairing, enjoyed the fruits of thrifty living. It was part of simplicity, something that I loved.

My experience of these testimonies shaped my life profoundly. To the extent that they rang true in practice, they laid a solid foundation. Where the practice was uneven, the dissonance raised up dilemma questions the search for whose answers provided a framework for my journey as an adult.

Quaker values and economics

But what does this experience of the Quaker testimonies have to do with economics? Well, everything, as it turns out.

It all started with integrity. A Quaker friend challenged me, well into my adulthood, to write a statement of conscience. She had been spending a lot of time helping young men who were struggling with the issue of conscientious objection to war. As they worked together on their statements of conscience, trying to articulate why they were choosing this path, she realized that this was a process we should all be engaged in. After all, conscience is not limited to people of a certain gender or a certain age.

Now this is a woman with a pretty forceful personality, and someone for whom I have a lot of respect. When she told me I should do this, I knew that there wasn't a viable alternative. So there I was, faced with the question: to what do I conscientiously object, and why?

It should have been a no-brainer. I came of age in the Vietnam War, went to my first big protest of many when I was a young teen, supported young Quaker men I knew who were agonizing over the draft. I remember when government agents came to a house where many of us were gathered, looking for resisters to arrest. We went together to court and jail.

But when I sat with this question, to what did I conscientiously object, it wasn't war that rose to the top. It was our economic system. I wrote: *I believe that a culture of economic materialism damages the soul and damages the fabric of society. It sets up a false god, squanders our resources, threatens our earth, distracts our attention from real issues and needs, and separates us from each other and from our higher selves.*

I closed with these words: *I could not participate in war. I could not imagine killing another human being. Both the teachings of Jesus and the tenets of Quakerism are blindingly clear on this point. But there is something about an economic system based on greed that seems even more evil than war. That system of domination is so inhuman, so antithetical to love or life. Its internal requirement, to accumulate profit and gain power regardless of the cost to humanity or the earth, sets us on the path to total destruction. It is the greatest evil that I know, and everything in me—by brain, my heart, my conscience—cries out against it.*

Economic issues pervade the testimonies. Quakers value equality, yet we see economic inequality increasing dramatically. We value integrity, yet our economic system has no place for conscience. We value simplicity, yet our growth economy requires ever-increasing consumption. We value community, yet our society throws out those on the margins. We value stewardship, yet are running through finite resources at an alarming rate. We value peace, yet the violence and devastation caused by our economic system's exploitation of people and the planet is tragic. Thus this walk through the Quaker testimonies with particular attention to our economic system.

Integrity

Friends, whatever ye are addicted to, the tempter will come in that thing; and when he can trouble you, then he gets advantage over you, and then you are gone. Stand still in that which is pure, after ye see yourselves; and then mercy comes in.
George Fox, 1652

Reflection: What rings true?

Every now and then I find myself engaged with life in a way that seems just right. I have a human interaction that is clear, connected, and deeply satisfying. I pause when I walk under a tree, taking in the colors, light and shadow that the sun and leaves create. I extend the life of something old and functional with a careful mend. I do a piece of work that matters and clearly has my name on it. I take the hard next step that's waiting to be taken in a friendship. I transplant a flower to give away, using my good compost. Something about what I'm doing rings true.

What rings true? I think this is a powerfully illuminating question to bring to all parts of our lives. When has my mind been clear? When have I made a decision or had an interaction, no matter how simple, that I'd be happy to live over and over again? What made that possible? When, in emotionally-charged mine-fields like relationships, gift-giving or eating, has a moment rung true? What made it right?

A bell can't ring true when it is covered or padded or stuffed. We have to get down to the bare bones of the matter. What clutters our minds? What messages have we taken in (from our childhoods, from advertising, from society at large) that muffle the truth? What has accreted to our social institutions that keeps us from discerning their true vocations? What layers of history and privilege and inequality obscure the possibility of respectful and mutual friendship in any situation?

Quaker John Woolman advises us to "Dig deep. ... Carefully cast forth the loose matter and get down to the rock, the sure foundation, and there hearken to the Divine Voice which gives a clear and certain sound."

What if the central principle for organizing our lives was moving ever closer to what rings true? It can be discouraging to notice how much of our time is spent elsewhere. We know that what we're doing doesn't ring true, but it's hard to see an alternative. Or we try to get some relief from that tinny sound with activities that are supposed to be pleasurable or comforting, but then those activities—often some form of addictive behavior— don't ring true either.

Just identifying this as something we want, however, and being able to recognize the moments when we've had it, is a big step forward. I smile as I imagine us counting up the minutes that ring true in our lives—just two minutes this day, maybe seven the next—and then reaching for more.

We don't have to just wait for a miracle to hear the ring of truth more often in our lives. We can remember those moments, and value them. We can look for where they most reliably occur. We can get help working to reproduce the conditions that encourage them. We can dig away at the stuff that muffles them. There may be no work that's harder—or more worth doing. And maybe, as we keep trying, it will get less hard—and we'll hear that ring of truth in our lives more often.

* * *

What rings true in the messages we get about ourselves as actors in our economic system? Much of it has a distinctly tinny sound: We need more stuff. Greed is good for us. Selfishness defines our essential nature and is the building block of a healthy economy. Advertisers help us secure the products that will make us happy. Well-being is most accurately measured in financial terms.

Competition brings out the best in us.

Going for the roots, where can we hear the ring of truth in ideas about what the economy is for? Is it for steadily increasing the power of the wealthiest? Maximizing profits by eliminating jobs that people need? Convincing us we need things we are better off without? Stripping the earth of resources and diminishing its ability to sustain life? Surely not.

The storyline of expanding opportunity, with rising tides lifting all boats, sounds a little better. Yet, as wealth has become steadily more concentrated at the top while more and more ordinary people struggle below, it has an increasingly hollow sound.

Where can we stand? The meaning of integrity centers around being sound and whole. Personal integrity calls for aligning our actions with our beliefs so they form one whole. Integrity of systems requires that all parts function together soundly, as a whole. Theologian Walter Wink contends that every human institution has a divine vocation, and the divine vocation of our economy is to provide for livelihood and welfare.

This aligns with the word's derivation: "eco" comes from the Greek "oikos," meaning an extended family unit, and "nomos" has to do with management. Thus, in its origins, economics meant the management of hearth and home. How do you manage a household with integrity? It is not hard to think of some basic approaches and values: know what is coming in and going out; don't take more than your share; take care of little and vulnerable ones; attend to cleaning; give up on things that are not working; don't focus on function at the expense of beauty; keep the long term in mind.

Widening our lens, we can notice places in our economic lives that have a ring of truth about them. A local credit union, a worker cooperative, a community supported agriculture scheme, a tool library—these are some of the building blocks of an economy with integrity.

The pursuit of integrity in the economic sphere requires us to keep several questions in front of us at once. How can we notice and build on those places that have the ring of truth? As we listen for that tinny sound, how can we face and name uncomfortable truths? And how can we do this both in our personal lives and in our wider communities?

In our personal lives

As a young adult, I was blessed to be part of a couple of religious and social change communities that took right relationship seriously. I got to experience simple community living, and engaging in "bread labor," part-time work that freed up time to pursue larger goals. We were all asking big questions about how the world worked, and how to do the right thing.

I remember the refrigerator question. Did I have a right to a refrigerator? There was no reason in the present to give it up, and I wasn't seriously considering it. But what if I came to the point where I felt that I couldn't do without one? If I believed that I was entitled to a refrigerator, would that someday put me on the wrong side of a struggle about equality and right sharing? Would I find myself protecting my possessions from those who had none? I still think it's a good question.

In an increasingly globalized economy, the question of complicity with injustice is everywhere. For just one example, consider the connection between our cell phones and warfare in eastern Congo. Profit from the mineral trade motivates and finances armed groups on all sides of the conflict there. Atrocities are used deliberately to intimidate local populations and secure control of mines and trading routes, causing the death of over five million people since 1998 — the largest documented death toll in the world since World War II. These minerals are critical in the manufacture of electronic devices — and those from the Congo are especially attractive because unregulated mining and cheap labor keep the costs down.

Are we ready to require that all the raw materials in our cell phones and computers be injustice-free—or give them up? Looking wider, consider that 40% of the people of Bangladesh live less than three feet above sea level, and it is the industrial West's level of consumption that is fueling global warming. How do we weed that out of our lives?

We need to come to terms with this hard truth: not only are we deeply complicit in war and injustice, but our best effort could never be enough to extract us from that complicity. It still makes sense to point ourselves in that direction—to live simply, to be willing to sacrifice convenience for the sake of right relationship, to keep alert to ways that we can disengage from evil. But perhaps our attention should be less on disengagement than on building our capacity for deep connection in the face of injustice—with our neighbors, with the people of Congo and Bangladesh, with our precious earth, with the Spirit that inhabits us all.

In our wider communities

Sometimes a community is faced with an issue of integrity that is as hard to navigate as the individual question of cell phones and atrocities in the Congo.

The umbrella organization for Quakers in the Philadelphia area had gone through some lean and painful years following the 2008 recession, laying off over a third of our staff and slashing program expenses to the bone. Finally, after several more years of tight fiscal controls, forced savings and austerity spending, at annual sessions in 2014, we heard the good news from our treasurer: Spending is stable; resources are up; income is showing a tendency to rise. If the stock market just continues to grow, we can anticipate more reassuring financial statements for years to come.

"If the stock market just continues to grow ..." That phrase rang in the ears of several of us who were active in our Friends Economic Integrity Project. What a paradox! We depend for our financial health on growth in the stock market. Yet that growth is a driver of economic inequality and environmental destruction.

Several of us gathered at the end of these sessions to scratch our heads together. With our organization's finances so deeply dependent on these investments, and many of us counting as never before on investment for our own retirement security, how could we challenge this system with integrity and effectiveness? To gather the will to make a transformative change, it seemed that we would have to break our dependence on financial speculation.

This dilemma is nested in a much larger one: How can we as individuals, families and communities make money decisions based on integrity when we are entangled in a system that fundamentally lacks it?

Those of us who gathered after sessions had many more questions than answers. But we knew they were important questions. We had a sense that recognizing and naming complicity was the first step in moving toward clarity and action. And we were willing to learn.

We do not live in a world that encourages us to listen to conscience. Yet, since conscience is one of the ways Spirit speaks to us, the more we listen the louder that voice will be. What would happen if we listened together more to where conscience might be leading us?

The things that are wrong in our economic system will never be changed until integrity is brought more fully to the public arena, and our values are on the table. Yet few of us feel that we belong. It helped me that my father was an economist, and the language of economics was in our house. I also witnessed a remarkable journey of integrity on his part. For decades he taught classical economics. His text that helped send all six of us to college was called *Money and Banking*. But in my teenage years I heard him questioning more and more the most basic tenets on which that theory was built, on which he had based his working life. His last decades were spent as an outspoken critic, calling the most fundamental assumptions of classical economics into question.

I had my struggles with my father, but this was a big gift. I learned that I had a right to look around this territory even without any formal training, a right to notice things that seemed inconsistent, a right to use the language, a right to ask questions.

I want everyone to feel that they have this right. Our world needs people of faith who are as outspoken about economics as Quakers are about war and peace. We are just not fooled when generals and politicians claim to be the experts about what will bring peace and security. We're ready to say that their expertise is based in flawed assumptions, and can never get us to peace. Even though we've never known a world without war, we hold to our beliefs, and are confident, outspoken and engaged.

Yet, when it comes to economists claiming to be the experts about what will bring prosperity, and advising us to leave the matter in their capable hands, we have tended to meekly comply. What would it be like to assert that their expertise is based on flawed assumptions that can never get the world to prosperity? Even though we've never known an economic system that works for everybody, we could hold to our deepest beliefs—that greed is not the source of well-being, and that unbridled growth comes at the expense of the planet's integrity—and be equally confident, outspoken and engaged.

What are the big values questions that need to be asked? Here are some that come to mind:

- What is true wealth? Is it the amount of money in our accounts? Is it the value of our infrastructure and what we produce, or our natural resources, or our fund of common knowledge, or our human capacity, or our spiritual depth? How can what we value be increased?
- What needs to be equal? Probably not everything—but some things.

- How do you track well-being? What do you measure?
- What does democracy have to do with economics? Who should decide, and where should control be located? There is probably no one answer for all situations, but it is a question that cries out to be asked.

Theologian Walter Wink sees Spirit at the core of every institution. These institutions, or Powers, he says, are created with the sole purpose of serving the general welfare of people and when they cease to do so, their spirituality becomes diseased. The task of the church is to identify these Powers, discern whether they contribute to the common good and if not, redeem them and call them back to their original "divine vocation."

Let's claim our right to do this, and bring our deepest faith values to the task. How has our economic system strayed from its divine vocation, and what do we want to call it back to?

Equality

That the sweat and tedious labor of the farmers, early and late, cold and hot, wet and dry, should be converted into the pleasure of a small number of men — that continued severity should be laid on nineteen parts of the land to feed the inordinate lusts and delicate appetites of the twentieth, is so far from the will of the great Governor of the world, ... [it] is wretched and blasphemous.
William Penn, 1669

Reflection: Meditations on Class

I had the unusual opportunity to be raised in an intentional community that was racially mixed, but solidly middle class. The adults around us knew enough to avoid racial stereotyping — which was an enormous gift — but they were not as aware about class. The plumber who made different spending choices from my Quaker parents, the girls from the trailer park down the road whose tight skirts and lipstick set them apart from us on the school bus, the mountain people who, for some unknowable reason, could never be part of our world — these were the people who were "other" in my childhood.

Yet is hard to have an "other" without a "better than," calling into question our deeply cherished belief in equality. The unity that is Gospel Order, or the Kingdom on Earth, requires everyone to be seen and known as God's children. The invisible walls that separate us from others also separate us from that beloved community.

Quakers who are comfortably white and middle class in the West (the experience from which I speak) often yearn for relationships with the oppressed. It's not surprising that we are drawn to those who have been badly treated. After all, that is our legacy. Our people were persecuted, and lived on the margins. Many of us have chosen the margins of our own culture, often believing that our faith requires that choice.

There is enormous power and liberation in claiming our right to relationship with people whom we've been taught were beyond reach. We assert our right to look for and find that of God in them, and our lives are richer as a result. I have experienced this in my diverse urban neighborhood. I love rubbing shoulders with my African American neighbors, with immigrants from Southeast Asia and West Africa. It makes me feel safer to not be so separated from people who are different from me. I can get to know human beings, and have some protection from the trap of believing that those differences are too great to be bridged.

Yet I find myself a little less eager, a little more defended, as I take on the challenge of reaching out and claiming white working-class folks. There is no lure of the exotic, just our own boring roots—and perhaps a reminder of the harshness from which we, or our families before us, worked hard to escape. In addition, for those who remain it can seem that the only way to handle that oppression is to create distance from the people who are even farther below, often minorities. It is hard to join with those whom we perceive as prejudiced, but in our eagerness to distance ourselves from them, are we any better?

How do we find our way? It won't be in trying harder to be good or do the right thing. It won't be in attempting to assuage guilt by vigorously taking up the causes of those less fortunate than ourselves. It will be in open-heartedly seeking that of God, not only in the most poor and oppressed, but in good religious conservatives, and hard-working loggers, and fierce protectors of the unborn, and passionate lovers of sports teams, and scared bread-winners who find their families on the edge. It will be in following our longing for connection with all of God's people.

* * *

The "better than/not as good as" frame, regardless of who we have been taught to put in which boxes, inevitably separates us from our fellow human beings and calls on us to internalize beliefs about ourselves that separate us from God. Yet an unshakeable confidence that we are all equal is hard to cultivate in an economic system in which resources are distributed so unequally, and which privileges those who have more. As I have sought to understand the dynamics of this aspect of our economy it has been sobering to discover how the system is hard-wired to increase inequality.

The connections between interest, debt and inequality are compelling. Since taking on loans means taking on debt, more money needs to be made in order to pay off the interest on that debt. And since for lenders, getting interest gives them more, while for debtors, paying back interest leaves them with less, there is built-in momentum toward inequality.

Sometimes a loan can be good for both sides. If you can rent some of my extra money to make even more, then we both come out ahead. But that doesn't seem to be the common situation among borrowers and lenders these days. The borrowers are mostly just struggling to stay even, and are often still falling behind. The lenders are steadily pulling away from the rest of the pack.

This raises big questions about fairness. Should it be easier for people with some assets to get more than for people with no assets to get some—and for others to work hard without getting any? What about student debt? Should people who have not yet begun their work life be in debt? When does having a debt become a life of indebtedness?

Then there are questions about rights. Do we have a right to interest income that we haven't worked for? It's easy to fault financial speculators who get obscenely wealthy making money off of money, but surely that's different from ordinary people like us who are just trying to save for retirement? Or is it? Beneath that question lies a bigger one: Does having something mean we have a right to it (and that gets back to my dilemma about the refrigerator)?

Ultimately there are questions about relationships, connection, and security. What if my gain in economic security involves someone else's loss? What does inequality—or even a focus on individual security—do to our sense of connection? What makes us safe? In the Christian tradition, the writers of the Gospels are pretty clear about the difference between financial and spiritual security. Matthew's admonition (6:19–21) to not store up treasures on earth, "for where your treasure is, there your heart will be also," rings with a warning for our time.

These questions are crying out to be asked in the public sphere, as the rich get richer and the poor get poorer, with minorities hit hardest of all; financial giants buy up, bleed dry and discard once-productive businesses that were the mainstay of communities; western nations extract wealth from their historic colonies while creating debt burdens that cripple entire countries.

To keep inequality from steadily increasing, strong countervailing public policies are required—and there is precedent for such policies. When I do workshops on leadership and advocacy with childcare workers, we talk about taxes as a source of revenue for socially beneficial goods and services, and I ask if anybody knows how much people in the US paid in taxes in the 1950s on income over $250,000. The guesses usually range from 5% to 20%. People are shocked when I share the real number: 91%. So back then, the idea was that $250,000 was enough, even for the rich. After you got that much money, it was rightly ordered that most of everything over that go back to the common pool for common needs.

Yet that all started to change in the late 1970s in the US and Britain. In the Reagan and Thatcher era, tax rates plummeted, regulations on business, banking and finance were loosened, and the private sector's influence grew. We are now seeing levels of inequality that boggle the mind. Oxfam reports that 82 percent of the wealth created in 2017 went to the top one percent of the global population!

It turns out that not only is this bad for the increasing number of people who struggle just to get by, it is bad for everybody in the country. According to Richard Wilkinson and Kate Pickett, authors of *The Spirit Level: Why More Equal Societies Almost Always Do Better*, when a variety of health and social problems are considered, outcomes are significantly worse in more unequal countries whether you are rich or poor. So, how can we pursue equality in economics both in our personal lives and in our wider communities?

In our personal lives

As we consider our personal finances, we can look for opportunities to participate in a shift toward greater equality. Is there income sharing that has our name on it, with people we know who lack resources through no fault of their own? What about reparations, and finding ways to redistribute some of what we have to groups that have been historically barred from accumulating assets?

We can reevaluate our roles as investors. It's good to invest, to put time, energy or resources into something in order to increase its value over time. We all invest in our families and communities. As teachers we invest in future generations. As farmers we invest in the soil. As citizens we invest in efforts to increase equity, justice and peace in the world around us.

But where our main goal is increased individual financial security, some distortions have crept in: We are using a proxy — money — for the thing we really value; we generally hand it over to somebody else to do the investing; and we have started to assume a right to receive back *more* than we put in.

Thinking individually about security is a recent phenomenon. Historically, we got our old age security by paying it forward; we tended aging parents with the expectation that our children, in turn, would care for us. More recently, governments have picked up some of the slack. It's only in the last several decades that we have moved to this individualized financial investment strategy, and the costs—to our personal integrity, to local economies and ecosystems, and to the health of our planet as a whole—are only beginning to be revealed.

Luckily, regardless of where we start, there is always a next step to take in the direction of aligning our investment practices more closely with our values. If our money is in speculative financial markets, we can choose greater social responsibility and screen out a variety of *negative* investments. For those who have already done this, we can choose for the type of *positive* production we are interested in supporting. A growing number of investment portfolios can help with this. Options are also growing for ordinary people to invest locally, in municipal bonds or community investment funds or even in specific sectors or businesses.

In a next step, we can put money in no-interest loans. Several platforms, like Kiva, now connect people of means with micro-financing projects around the world, supporting the livelihoods of others who have little access to capital.

We can go farther and reframe our whole idea of security, from individual financial savings for an uncertain future to building the larger community's capacity to meet its common needs. This could involve divesting ourselves of excess income and redirecting it toward our faith communities, toward efforts to increase the social safety net, toward groups working for increased equity and poverty reduction, toward local food security efforts, toward global sustainability.

In our wider communities

There are a variety of community practices around money that tend toward greater equality. I know of families and religious communities that have chosen to buy up student loans and credit card debt from their members and set up loan repayment agreements with zero or minimal interest rates. Some religious communities are experimenting with "pay as led" financing for their gatherings.

Credit unions are a wonderful institution where debt and interest stay in the same closed local system. I was so happy to take my money out of the big bank in our city and put it all in our local credit union. If I borrow money there, I am borrowing from my neighbors. If I have money there in savings it is being used to support my neighbors. (I keep wishing I had the time and energy to organize local members to run for places on the credit union board, to make the concept of community-ownership a little more real—but that's another story ...)

We can put our weight behind practices that pull down the accumulation of excessive wealth. Some cities are passing ordinances that add a tax to corporations whose CEOs make more than 100 times the average of their workers. (In 1965 the average in the US was 20-to-1; by 2013 it was almost 300-to-1.) We can support bills to end preferential tax treatment for wealthy hedge fund managers. Some are working toward a financial transaction tax—or "Robin Hood Tax"—which would take a tiny bite out of each computerized transaction on the financial markets, as a way to discourage making money from money without contributing anything to the real economy.

Similarly, we can put our weight behind policies to pull people up out of oppressive debt. There are a daunting number of opportunities here: around payday lending practices, credit card fees, student debt, underwater mortgages, and probably more.

We can keep in mind the systemic racism that has been present in asset-building since the dawn of colonialism in general and US slavery in particular, and can have an eye out for policies that are not just race-neutral, but that actively help level the playing field.

We can support the kind of government policies that once helped grow the middle class, whose prospects have been steadily eroded by the resurgence of private sector control. Opportunities here include efforts to raise the minimum wage; greater public support for college education; a revised personal income tax structure (could the US ever get back to that 91 percent?); affordable health insurance; perhaps even a guaranteed income. Thinking even bigger, we can support the idea of moving our whole money creation system out of the for-profit banking sector, and back into the public sector.

Then there is debt jubilee. All major religions had strong early prohibitions against usury and a strong concern about debt. From the ancient Near East to the tribes of Israel, to Germany after World War II, debt forgiveness has been used to restore balance, get people back on their feet and sustain economic health. The global Jubilee 2000 campaign led to the cancellation of more than $100 billion of debt owed by 35 of the world's poorest countries—a move that appeared to have no losers. Forgiving debt is a powerful way to address inequality, and one that is certainly basic to Christianity, as we call on God to "forgive us our debts, as we also have forgiven our debtors."

Simplicity

It is our tender and Christian advice that Friends take care to keep to truth and plainness, in language, habit, deportment and behavior; that the simplicity of truth in these things may not wear out nor be lost in our days.
Yearly Meeting in London, 1691

Reflection: The Big Addiction

Imagine the old temperance fighters, denouncing drink in the strongest language they could find: There is a great evil abroad in our land. It coarsens the spirit, deadens the soul. It threatens the health and stability of the family and leads our youth astray. As surely as night follows day, it will destroy the lives of all who give over their will and succumb to its lures.

There is indeed a great evil abroad in our land. More dangerous by far than alcohol, it is the evil of materialism. The meaning and power are being sucked out of countless lives and replaced with stuff. Our loved ones are being snatched away into some kind of a demonic cult, being brainwashed into worshiping Mammon, blindly seeking salvation through the latest fashion or newest model. Yet there are more people in this cult than outside of it. Like the worst horror movie, our whole society is becoming possessed.

Just as fascination with pornography is a passive, addictive, and ultimately unfulfilling substitute for intimacy, so is fascination with consumption a passive, addictive, and ultimately unfulfilling substitute for being present to the challenges and opportunities of the world around us. We're stuffing ourselves, and keep reaching for more, because we're starving for the real thing.

This is an addiction that gets into our blood without us even realizing. So just starting to notice the signs is an important first step toward regaining control. When that little rush of good feeling that comes with buying something makes me want more, I am addicted. When shopping or consuming entertainment seem like the best solution to a certain flatness in life, I am duped and deluded. When a clever advertisement has me reaching for my wallet, I am manipulated. When being without a certain item makes me feel vulnerable, isolated, less sure of myself, or left behind, I am imprisoned. When I feel compelled to acquire or consume, I am enslaved.

This is not just a harmless habit or an occasional lapse of judgment. We're talking about our whole society being duped and deluded, manipulated, drugged and addicted, imprisoned and enslaved—and most of us don't even know it. To offer a challenge is tricky, because some amount of material goods, like some amount of food and water, actually sustain life. We can't completely do without the way you can with alcohol or drugs.

To armor ourselves against this siren call, we have to remember: I am completely beautiful in the eyes of God. Nothing I buy has the power to change who I am. The soul cannot be fed by stuff. Precious moments cannot be bought or sold. Enough is enough.

* * *

While materialism can be framed as a spiritual issue, it turns out to be a critical ingredient of a growth-based economy as well. Since most of our money is created through interest-bearing loans—or debt—more money needs to be continually made in order to pay off the interest on that debt. To create demand for a growing market, more people need to be steadily convinced that they need more things. Thus the requirement for economic growth is baked into the system.

When there were great untapped resources—minerals, forests, topsoil—and easy access to stored sunlight from the past in fossil fuels, such an expansive system could be a rough fit with our planet. But that is no longer the case. How can we reconcile growth and a finite planet?

Reflection: Growth dilemmas

It's hard not to have a love-hate relationship with growth. On the one hand, everybody wants things to grow. We nurture little children, coax seedlings into healthy plants, incubate new businesses, invest in emerging talents with the hopes that they will make it big time.

Yet growth can be problematic. If something is good, more of it is not necessarily better. My six-foot-five son was relieved when he finally stopped getting taller. Enormous impersonal consolidated schools are now being broken up into smaller units more conducive to human interaction and learning. And we would do anything to stop those cancer cells from growing.

How do we balance these two truths about growth? It's easiest with children—and other living things—where we don't have much control. They will grow, for the most part, until they are at their mature size, and then they'll stop. Some mysterious internal mechanism knows when they are big enough, when more growth would actually hinder their long-term ability to survive.

But with our human-made institutions, we have no such internal regulator, and our deeply culturally-embedded belief that bigger must be better is getting us into more and more trouble. Nowhere is this more true than in the economy, where growth has become enshrined as a central, unquestionable, quasi-religious, belief. Our well-being, we are told, is dependent on an ever-growing economy: more markets, more consumption, more record highs in the financial markets.

Yet this economic system is looking less and less like a little child who needs to grow, and more and more like a seven-foot person who's having trouble fitting into ordinary spaces and showing no signs of slowing down—more and more like a cancer growing out of control.

The idea of continuous growth inevitably runs into the limits of the system that contains it. Our growth economy is running through the stored wealth of a finite planet, paying dividends in the present by running up debts against the future, while becoming ever less effective in meeting people's real needs. It is threatening integrity on all fronts, eating up poor people to feed the wealthy, eating up Main Street to feed the financial sector, eating up the biosphere to feed the GNP. We find ourselves in the surreal situation of being strong-armed into spending ever more money on things we don't really need in order to keep afloat a system that has become unmoored from reality and common sense.

Luckily growth doesn't just have to be about getting bigger. After all, we have confidence that our children can continue to grow after they reach their full height. We look forward to them becoming smarter, more able, more mature, even wiser. It's harder with the economy. We've accepted growth in this area as a good thing for so long that it seems like a law of nature. But nature is crying out against it, and what we have made, we can change. (Though our economic high priests could use some help from ordinary folks here—like the child who pointed out that the emperor had no clothes.) We can trade in this outmoded model centered on bigger for one centered on smarter. We can cut out the cancerous growth, lean into our values around simplicity, and start learning all the joys as well as the challenges of finding our place within the constraints of a finite planet.

In our personal lives

In this context, being content with enough is a revolutionary act. Yet, when we have easy access to more than we need, how can we tell when it's enough? I experimented with this concept recently when I was trying to lose some weight. I filled a glass of water, took one tasty little cracker and proceeded to eat it, very slowly. It *was* tasty—every single tiny little bite. I felt like I'd given myself the full cracker experience, with hardly any carbs. Similarly, a single chocolate chip can provide a powerful long-lasting chocolate taste.

Even though the quantities are much smaller, I am getting the same amount of enjoyment out of things that I love—or maybe even more—simply by putting more attention to enjoying them—and I'm losing weight! Of course we may well be more motivated to lose excess weight than excess shoes, or excess hours of being entertained. But I think the principle is the same.

If we can't pay attention to enjoying what we already have, then going for more is probably a waste of resources—because we'll keep seeking fulfillment through the getting rather than the enjoying, and it will never feel like enough. This is bad for our own well-being and, multiplied by millions of fulfillment seekers, bad for the future of our spaceship earth.

Some people in this world don't have enough to lead decent healthy lives and really do need more. But for many of us, the path to feeling like we have enough lies more in our attitude and where our attention goes than in greater consumption. Maybe we'd actually be helped by more scarcity—if we don't have much, then our only path to happiness is to enjoy it a lot!

In our wider communities

To the extent that we can share with others, our individual needs are lessened. There are many possibilities here. Just as access to a local library means we don't have to own books to get their value, access to a tool library, for example, means we don't have to own a tool to use it. A community that shares values around simplicity has the additional advantage of helping to buffer us from the lures of consumerism and create a different definition of what is "normal." Such a community is more likely to value other simplifying alternatives, such as time and skill shares and home-made play and entertainment. In an unexpected benefit, as we find ways to reduce our needs, the time and money that are freed up often open doors to new options and possibilities.

In the public arena, anything to mitigate the forces that have us accumulating more than we need will help. Reining in the shamelessly manipulative advertising industry is an obvious one. Undercutting the fear-based impulse to hoard for a rainy day—through providing public assurance that our most basic needs will be met—is another. (An experiment with guaranteed income in Manitoba, Canada had few discernible downsides, and was astonishingly effective.)

There is growing interest around the world in rethinking how we measure our economy's health. Focusing less on output and more on human well-being would be a powerful support for cultivating the joys of simple living. I've never heard anyone talk about this more eloquently than Robert F. Kennedy:

The gross national product includes air pollution and advertising for cigarettes, and ambulances to clear our highways of carnage. It counts locks for our doors, and jails for the people who break them.

And if the gross national product includes all this, there is much that it does not comprehend. It does not allow for the health of our families, the quality of their education, or the joy of their play. It does not include the beauty of our poetry or the strength of our marriages, the intelligence of our public debate or the integrity of our public officials. ...

It measures neither our wit nor our courage, neither our wisdom nor our compassion. It measures everything, in short, except that which makes life worthwhile.

Reflection: Wealth and poverty

When you travel from the richest country in the Americas to one of the poorest, the issue of wealth and poverty cannot be avoided.

Yet in a way, they are very relative terms.

Visiting my son in Nicaragua, I stayed in a quiet neighborhood in a mid-sized city. Streets were cleaned and trash was collected. You could count on regular morning delivery of newspapers, milk and fuel. There were convenient corner stores, the outdoor market had a great supply of fruits and vegetables, and the supermarket was within walking distance. Inexpensive taxis and cheaper public transportation were easily available. Our house had electricity, a stove and refrigerator, bathroom and laundry as well as ample living and sleeping space, all surrounding a beautiful patio. Computer access was convenient and cheap. People worked and went to school, laughed and played, and hung out with family and friends. It was safe to be out at night. All in all, it was a very livable city.

From the perspective of Western wealth, however, the place was impossible. Public transportation was a fleet of decrepit school buses cast off from wealthier nations, and microbuses into which people were shoehorned till there was barely space to breathe. Many families' vehicle was a bicycle—carrying two, and often three, people. Our diet was a variation on beans and rice, the toilets couldn't handle toilet paper, the water ran only erratically, clothes were washed by hand, and you had to go to a cyber-cafe to check your e-mail. Work was hard to come by, signs of poverty were everywhere, and the heat was incredible.

It would be very good for this city to have more wealth, but it doesn't need to be transformed to a western model to be a good place to live. And the fact that it does work calls into question some of our assumptions about the good life.

Are washing machines and twenty-four hour running water necessary for our well-being? Are we deprived without video games and an infinite choice in food products? Is it so bad to spend free time in the evening sitting out on the step with our neighbors? Do we all need our own cars and computers and air-conditioning to survive?

As we move toward the end of the cheap fossil fuel era, our wealthy countries are going to face increasingly hard choices. We may need to study the models of livable neighborhoods and communities in poor countries as we consider how to retool our lives. Perhaps what we have to give up will turn out to be excess—stuff we never really needed in the first place.

* * *

The Quaker testimony on simplicity provides strong support for just saying no, for choosing *against* the drumbeat of materialism, and *for* the non-material inputs that are more likely to meet real needs. Living out our values around simplicity with all the intention and power we can muster—and sharing the joy of that choice with others—is part of calling the economy back to its divine vocation of providing for human welfare on a finite earth.

Stewardship/Regeneration

The produce of the earth is a gift from our gracious creator to the inhabitants, and to impoverish the earth now to support outward greatness appears to be an injury to the succeeding age.
John Woolman, 1772

Reflection: Mastery

Mastery seems to be something we as human beings take to naturally. As children we are deeply and innately engaged in mastery—first of our internal functions, then of mobility and speech, and then of whatever else we have access to. In our school years we have the opportunity to master more skills and information. Our entire childhood is one great exercise in self-mastery.

We can see mastery in the history of our species as well. When we learned to plant crops, there came the opportunity to settle down and store a little extra, freeing up some members of the community to engage in activity separate from survival. More and more inquiring minds gathered more and more information about the world, leading to the explosion of knowledge of the Scientific Revolution, and our current belief that we are infinitely capable of mastering all aspects of life on this planet.

It's not surprising that a little mastery gives us a taste for more, nor that such a desire can be abused. We see this directly when one person or group exercises mastery over another—in child or spousal abuse, in enslavement, colonization, and dictatorship. We see it more subtly in how advertisers master psychology to sell us their products, or how spin doctors master the presentation of information to suit their ends. What is natural and benign in an infant's exploration of self becomes problematic when this power is exercised over another.

Perhaps even more problematic for the future of our species

is the idea that we can be masters over the earth itself. As we've come close to making our planet uninhabitable in this endless lust for mastery over, we may finally be realizing that stronger forces are at work here, that the earth needs our species less than we need the earth. As we reach that limit of mastery over, we may be in a teachable moment, with the opportunity to learn self-mastery in a whole new way.

An understanding is growing among us that our species is inextricably intertwined with innumerable others that, together with the earth, make up the web of life that supports us all. In that way, we are one body. And like a child that has just been born, advanced western civilization doesn't have much experience with this body. We're just learning how it works as a single system in a way that supports life in the long term—and we have much less control than we would wish.

Now here is a situation crying out for self-mastery—and the good news is that the untapped potential is enormous. So long as we can remember that we're one body, the likelihood of abuse drops, while endless vistas of opportunities for self-mastery—more than the most adventurous infant could hope for—open up before us.

* * *

I include **stewardship** dutifully in the list of Quaker testimonies, but have growing reservations about the whole concept. If our goal is a relationship of integrity with the world around us, then we'll certainly have to give up the frame of mastery over and everything that goes with it—domination, control, warfare and subjugation—but stewardship won't quite get us there either.

A steward, says the dictionary, is one who manages another's affairs, usually with their best interest in mind. The relationship is not inherently conflicted, as it is with mastery; good stewards of the earth are more likely to put effort into caring for it than exploiting it. But the separation remains. As a steward, I act not on my own behalf, but on behalf of another. The assumption lingers that the steward is not part of the other, and the steward knows best. Slaveholders who considered themselves enlightened may well have embraced the concept of stewardship of their property.

The end point has to be reclaiming our connection with and belonging to the community of life on Earth. Just as our families and our people are part of the larger body that we claim as ours, so are we part of an even larger body, the biosphere. When we can know this truth deep in our bones, then we are no longer stewards looking on or over. We are members, looking out from within.

Fortunately, our Quaker testimonies are not set in stone, and we stand by our belief in continuing revelation. If we find the concept of stewardship too constraining, we can search for a framework that provides better guidance in the twenty-first century. I am excited about the concept of "regeneration." Not only does it move us from problematic frames of superiority and separation, but it squarely puts forth the challenge of supporting life and the creative process in all parts of our lives and the environment around us, including our economy.

Reflection: Extract or generate?

When people talk about our economic system, the traditional insider language is about free markets, free enterprise, free trade, the invisible hand, the profit motive, supply and demand. Critics use different—and often stronger—language: runaway capitalism, unbridled profiteering, greed-based driver of inequality, the corporate state. But until recently, I'd never heard our economy characterized as "extractive," and that term has gotten me thinking.

There's something about it that rings very true. We pride ourselves on the amount of minerals and fossil fuels that we can extract from beneath the earth's crust. We extract maximum value from the topsoil and the forests and the oceans. Employers typically have a goal of extracting ever more work from their employees. Financial institutions prosper when they extract maximum profit from every transaction—ATM withdrawals, credit card charges, mortgage rates, currency exchange interactions, and things most of us don't even understand, like credit swaps, hedges and derivatives. The goal in each case is maximum extraction for maximum profit. The losers, clearly, are ordinary people, the earth, and other living things.

The alternative would be a "generative" economy. I looked this word up to make sure I knew what it meant, and found definitions involving the power or function of generating, originating, producing, creating. Where there wasn't anything before, there is now something new.

In our personal lives

Generative. My mind goes immediately to the soil. I was picking lettuce not long ago, getting ready to make lunch, and noticed a little dirt at the base of a leaf. I rubbed it off, but didn't even bother to wash it. After all, that was dirt that had been created in my compost pile, and I knew all the good ingredients that had gone into it. I love generating soil for my garden. There is some necessary extraction of nutrients as the plants grow, but with compost continually added, it just keeps getting richer and richer. Overall, my little agricultural system is far more generative than extractive.

There are many other places in our lives where this distinction might apply. We can extract productivity from those who work under us or generate loyalty and trust. We can extract obedience from children or generate a spirit of mutual cooperation. We can extract the benefits of a nice neighborhood or well-functioning religious congregation for ourselves or put energy into generating benefits for the whole. We can extract entertainment from an outside source or generate fun for ourselves and others. We can extract the maximum value out of any connection to serve our own ends, or focus on the opportunity it brings to generate new possibilities or relationships.

I'm deeply committed to building the power and the will to challenge our extractive economy, from curbing fossil fuel extraction to taming multinational corporations to taxing speculative financial transactions that maximize profit without increasing our community well-being. I'm also committed to supporting new economic institutions that help build up a generative economy—coops of all kinds; credit unions; community gardens; enterprises that embrace the triple bottom line of profit, people, and planet.

As I continue to find my place in such efforts, however, I don't have to wait. I can consider my own life choices and notice where I am extracting as a citizen, family member, worker and consumer, and where I am generating new wealth, resources and possibilities. As I notice, I can shift my weight toward a more generative economy.

In our wider communities

Embracing the challenge of generation and regeneration rather than extraction requires not just committing to sustain what currently exists, but supporting new and renewed life. In the process, it requires rethinking our whole economic model.

Since the Enlightenment and the Scientific and Industrial Revolutions, we have tended to think in a linear model: progress, knowledge, mastery of the environment, and humanity in general are all on an upward trajectory. The line moves steadily forward and always up.

Our production systems conform to that same linear model: extract, produce, consume, discard, leaving a trail of waste all along the way. Since natural resources, fossil fuels, and the capacity of the earth to absorb waste have all seemed unlimited until very recently, this approach has appeared straightforward and totally logical. As we begin to get our minds around the startling new idea that the economy does not exist in some independent and separate sphere, but is, in fact, embedded in an ecosystem, and a finite ecosystem at that, we start to see the necessity of moving toward a model more in line with natural systems—one that is more circular than linear.

This would mean creating systems of production where all the by-products, whether in the form of energy or matter, are put to use. As opposed to the extract/produce/consume/discard system that follows the more linear "cradle to grave" model, this is a circular "cradle to cradle" model. Examples of organizing production in this way can be seen in aquaponics systems, in the recyclable carpet industry, and in wool production that generates potable wastewater and mulch, to name just a few.

Another way of focusing on renewing life is shifting from valuing obsolescence to valuing durability. If a company assumes responsibility for on-going maintenance of their product, a strong incentive is created to build to last, and employment is generated in maintenance, repair and recycling of a durable stock of goods. Our whole perspective begins to shift from production of goods to production of services.

The opportunities to live out a testimony on regeneration in our communities are enormous. Because most ecosystems are local, most life-creating and life-renewing initiatives are likely to be locally based as well. Think community gardens, farmers markets and consumer sponsored agriculture schemes, compost pick-up services, community solar, land trusts, businesses using local products and local talent, community repair and weatherization projects, open land planning, tool libraries, time banks, community theaters. The possibilities are endless.

As we think about larger policies and power shifts, at least three broad approaches come into focus: squeeze the space where extraction is the dominant mode; expand the space for generation and regeneration; and hold out possibilities for renewing life.

To squeeze the extraction sector, we can be alert for possibilities to rein in the now virtually unfettered corporations, i.e., measures to rule that they are not people and cannot expect to enjoy the rights of people, challenging their immunity to local law, and punishing them for law-breaking as we punish people. We could learn from the model in some European countries where all stakeholders, including workers and community members, sit on corporate boards.

Another avenue is to create tax, incentive, and regulatory structures to encourage truly sustainable production technologies. Higher taxes at points of extraction and waste and the removal of hidden (or sometimes not so hidden) subsidies to agribusiness and the fossil fuel and nuclear power industries could even out the playing field in ways that would encourage more sustainable farming and technologies. Companies could be made responsible for disposal of the products they sell, or for their repair. Recycling regulations could be made stricter. Advertising could be more closely regulated, more heavily taxed, or simply curtailed.

To expand the space for regenerative economic activity, government can encourage and protect other ownership and production models, such as small businesses, benefit corporations, cooperatives and land trusts. The growing rights of nature movement can be supported. The principle in Catholic social thought of subsidiarity, which holds that nothing should be done by a larger and more complex organization which can be done as well by a smaller and simpler one, can be held up. Much economic innovation is happening these days at the local level, and those spaces need to be both protected and expanded.

To find our way to a public mindset of regeneration, we are going to need new models and images. I have found unexpected help in the unlikely metaphor of agricultural drainage ditches. It seems that modern practice is to try to drain water off of fields as efficiently as possible, which means making deep and straight ditches that lead directly to a bigger waterway. But it turns out that deep and straight ditches are also efficient in washing away topsoil, eroding banks, and sending agricultural poisons directly into the adjacent water supplies. It turns out that, if you're thinking in terms of the health of the ecosystem, it's better to have a very slow and meandering stream that takes its time, replenishes the surroundings, and does a lot of self-cleaning in the process.

This is probably not an exact metaphor, but I'm pretty sure that healthy production eco-systems—and financial ecosystems as well—would be slow. There would not be an efficient stream whose goal was to pour the maximum amount of stuff and profits out at the end. Rather, as its resources meandered and percolated through the local economy, the health of the local system would be steadily replenished.

This brings up the related question of what I can learn about being "a channel of God's peace." Being a channel requires maintaining a flow, so it makes sense to put attention to clearing away obstructions. But should my goal be efficiency, on the model of those modern agricultural drainage ditches? If I work to get my channel straight and well-lined, will God's peace flow through more quickly and easily? Or would I be of better service as the meandering kind, with more slow-moving opportunities for peace to soak in around me? Somehow I doubt if I'll find the final word here. But following this thread of curiosity and wonder has made me smile more than once. And I do trust the wisdom of eco-systems—which may be all the answer I need.

Peace

We utterly deny all outward wars and strife and fightings with outward weapons, for any end, or under any pretense whatsoever; and this is our testimony to the whole world ... [W]e do certainly know, and so testify to the world, that the spirit of Christ, which leads us into all Truth, will never move us to fight and war against any man with outward weapons, neither for the kingdom of Christ, nor for the kingdoms of this world.
Declaration of Friends to Charles II, 1660

Reflection: Peace Connection

When I was growing up, peace was a divisive issue. World War II was a fresh memory, our country was in the throes of the Cold War, and anybody who wasn't prepared to take a stand against the Communists was seen as a weakling if not a threat to our way of life. When I was a child, I remember the mother of one of my Quaker friends protesting against the air raid drills that happened in our town. When we were all supposed to be inside, practicing being safe, she went parading around in public carrying an umbrella, suggesting that her umbrella was about as good a protection against nuclear war as all the safeguards our town officials were so determined to enact. She got arrested and spent a night in jail, as I'm sure she had intended, and life went on. I remember being torn between the moral necessity of supporting her action, as part of our Quaker Peace Testimony, and an acute awareness that everyone else around us thought she was being ridiculous.

I can't remember when I first learned those words of early Friends to King Charles: "We utterly deny all outward wars and strife and fighting with outward weapons for any end or under any pretense whatever." This is stirring sentiment, to be sure, but so uncompromising. What space did it leave you for connecting with the rest of the world?

In a way, the opportunity to protest the Vietnam War as a teenager was a welcome relief to me. Finally I could see the Peace Testimony as more than just a moral imperative to do a deeply unpopular thing. Rather, with the war seeming so unjust and wrong, it undergirded our natural inclinations to speak out. We could play a significant role in getting the opposition in motion, then, as the years went on, had the thrill of seeing more and more people join in. For the first time in my life, standing for peace was not pitting me and my little group against the rest of the world.

But it was only with an action a little later, one that probably most people have never heard of, that I got the taste of the possibility of deeper connection. When US military equipment destined for West Pakistan in support of its war with East Pakistan (now Bangladesh) was being loaded onto ships in 1971, a small flotilla of Quakers in canoes and kayaks tried to stop the ships. At first this little threat was easily turned away, but then the Quakers were able to find an ally among the longshoremen at the Port of Philadelphia who brokered the union's support. When the next ship pushed off, no cargo had been loaded or unloaded. After four more months of intense protests—and picketing in front of the White House—the US government finally ended all arms exports to Pakistan. It was the connection between the Quakers and longshoremen that spoke to me.

In the early 1980s, I had a similar experience with the Jobs with Peace campaign. Part of a national campaign (full of Quakers, I'm sure), we worked in Philadelphia on a referendum asking that more federal funds be made available for local jobs and services by reducing military spending beyond the defensive needs of the nation. I remember our cramped office in the corner of a union hall, and deciding to give away half of an unexpected little legacy from my father to help fund outreach in the working-class districts of the city. When the referendum passed by an almost three-to-one margin, I was thrilled to feel connected with all those people throughout the city, from all walks of life, who were ready to challenge our leaders' assumptions about what created the conditions for peace.

Finally, now I could link peace with justice. Now I could talk confidently with anyone about the impact that war and preparation for war has on people's lives. It didn't have to be an individual moral stand that separated me from the rest of the world. I'm not sure what George Fox, with his utter denial of all outward strife, would think, but I had found my way to a peace testimony that worked for me.

* * *

Peace is increasingly hard to come by these days. We are on the cusp of a new era, entering into a chaotic time of transition—where fossil fuels will no longer provide us with cheap energy and the environment is tipping into disequilibrium; where our economic system no longer reliably delivers wealth to anybody but the rich; where wars have become unwinnable and civilians do most of the suffering. People with anything to lose are scared, desperately clutching at a past that is slipping out of their grip. Fears are driving hateful and violent rhetoric that indicates a willingness to discard whole groups of people. This era of heightened protectionism, gated communities, and soaring prison populations increases suspicion and hyper-vigilance that make nobody safe.

Despite the traditional anti-war weight of our Peace Testimony, being for peace has to be so much more than being against war. There can be no true peace in a context of violence or in the absence of justice, even if no war has been declared or no traditionally-recognizable conflict is visible.

Our economic system is steeped in violence. Coal companies' practice of cutting off mountain tops, destroying forests, polluting waterways, threatening the livelihood of whole communities is perceived as sound business practice in pursuit of legitimate profit. Gouging poor people with extortionate interest rates is identified as smart niche marketing. Buying up healthy companies for short-term profit, bleeding them dry and throwing them and their communities away results in fat bonuses for CEOs.

Furthermore, many of the wars in which we play a role have deep economic roots. I remember a telling sign from a demonstration against the war in Iraq: "What is *our* oil doing under *their* sand?" How much of war is fueled by inequality and the demands of a growth economy in a world of increasing scarcity? How much is it fueled by a desire to gain greater control over wealth or productive assets or water? Removing economic injustice from that picture would certainly drain a lot of conflict.

In our personal lives

Many of us who value peace have deeply internalized the central Quaker tenet of that of God in everyone. We know that doing violence to others damages us all. We strive to be peaceable in our daily lives. Yet this laudable intention is often coupled with highly developed skills in conflict avoidance—and we would do well to notice that a preference for avoiding conflict can't help but serve the status quo more than it serves the forces of change.

I am one of these people, and I keep trying to get my mind more fully around the concept of conflict as a positive and healthy opportunity for growth. Quaker nonviolent strategist and trainer George Lakey has helped me here. When everything is in motion, he says, there is room for change. Molecules move more freely in a context that is hot than in one that is cold. Things can be rearranged. New patterns can emerge. Conflict warms us up. It makes available things that are otherwise very hard to achieve. The violence is already there, embedded deep in structures of injustice. We're just raising it to the surface so that what was frozen in place can be transformed.

Just committing to believing this is a good first step. There are many other steps we can take: noticing where we have engaged in conflict and survived; learning when and how our fears about conflict come up, and finding ways to blunt their impact or dilute their strength; celebrating the tiniest successes; making opportunities to be around people who are good at conflict, and learning from them.

We can also consider the internal implications of disarmament. Many of us would readily agree that arming ourselves tends to make us less safe at all levels. An international arms race adds to the danger of war. Developing the hardware that makes indiscriminate tackles in sports acceptable increases the incidence of concussion. Having guns in the home makes gun deaths there more likely.

Arming ourselves also ties up resources that could be used to grow the conditions for peace and justice. Gated communities sidestep the need to address inequity. Those with a militant theology or world view create an "other" against whom constant vigilance is required. Those who are armed with hate have less space for love.

Yet how many of us are good at disarming ourselves? I remember the shock of discovering this irony—that we can blithely and righteously call for nations to lay down their arms, thus increasing their vulnerability to attack, when we would never consider giving up the defenses that we've built up internally. Is there any one of us without elaborate defense systems—against insult or failure, humiliation or loss? Yet, if I am armed to the teeth internally, how can I demand that others lay down their arms? I need to practice the courage of being vulnerable, of living an ever-more undefended life, of opening myself to all these potentially devastating blows, before I can preach with integrity to the nations.

In our wider communities

There are many ways of attending in our communities to

those who have experienced violence, listening for links with the economic system, and putting our resources toward a just peace. On a broader scale, probing for and talking about the economic roots of conflict and war may bring additional allies who are not swayed by moral arguments alone. Talking about the cost of preparation for war, and all that could be done for our communities with a reduction of military budgets (and how profit-seeking corporations are the big winners in those budgets) can also expand our reach. We can be clear that no lasting peace is possible without justice. In the domestic "wars" that our nations take on (wars on drugs, wars on terror) we can do the same.

As we learn to talk about peace and economics in the same breath, new possibilities open up. I continue to be inspired by the story of how the concern of a handful of Quakers about militarism grew into a program that now provides fresh organic produce to more than half of the state of New Mexico's school children. Through the story run strands of deep listening, respect for indigenous spirituality, and a vision of an economy and a land that nurtures the community's well-being.

Back in the 1970s, a group of Quakers in northern New Mexico asked the American Friends Service Committee (AFSC) to help address the tilt toward militarism in the economy around the nuclear weapons labs of Los Alamos. Rather than just jumping in with a focus on peace, the AFSC did a listening project in the wider community. Over and over again they heard concern from the indigenous people, the Pueblos, not about militarism, but about land and water rights. They heard the underlying spiritual principle, that the water belongs to the earth and the earth belongs to God—and they followed the community's lead.

After working for twenty-five years to protect land grant communities and empower regional associations of community-based irrigation systems that have provided water to agricultural communities for the last four hundred years, the AFSC program in New Mexico turned its attention toward the land. How might traditional land use systems and values best be supported in the twenty-first century?

They chose to support sustainable agriculture practices, already so deeply embedded in the culture, by training new farmers and developing cooperative marketing systems. Over the years, this has resulted in scores of new farmers, technical support for over a hundred small farms, and three farmer cooperatives. Many older people who can no longer work the land are now able to maintain their water rights, and young people in a region of high unemployment have new livelihoods.

To secure land and water rights and ongoing employment requires stable markets for farm produce. So the project advocated for the state to fund publicly-supported schools to purchase local produce for their feeding programs. This resulted in the school districts receiving thousands of dollars to pay for school lunch ingredients from local farmers. Staff have helped the farmer cooperatives negotiate initial contracts with the school districts, and worked to create a network of cooperatives across New Mexico. As the coop members learn these aspects of the business, the AFSC is steadily working itself out of a job.

One native Pueblo requested AFSC's assistance but did not want to be involved with the market economy at all. With many elders and unemployed youth, they asked for help obtaining a large passive solar hoop house that would permit year-round food production. AFSC found a donor to purchase the materials and then trained a group of youth from the tribe to construct it. The beds were raised high enough that the older people could have access to them. Thus youth gained construction and farming skills and elders got good nutritious food without any money changing hands.

In much of New Mexico agriculture is culture, and culture is rooted in spiritual practice. The AFSC walks with the people on the saint day of farmers, as the community blesses the fields and the water blesses the community, in a mutually respectful and public blend of indigenous and Catholic traditions.

People feel supported in their traditional spirituality and connection to the land. They are heartened by new possibilities, and have not failed to notice that the coops provide an important economic alternative to low-wage jobs or military and border patrol service. And what about those peace-minded Quakers, who originally petitioned for the AFSC to come in to the area to address the problem of militarism? They learned that by listening deeply and following where you are led, your dreams can come true—in the most unexpected and soul-nourishing ways.

Community

Our life is love and peace and tenderness, and bearing one with another, and not laying accusations one against another; but praying one for another, and helping one another up with a tender hand.
Isaac Penington, 1667

Reflection: Leaving the Land of I

It didn't take a Kansas tornado for us to find ourselves in the Land of I. Many of us were born there and have lived there all our lives, not knowing any other place as home. For others our homeland has been transformed so gradually that it's been hard to notice the change from day to day. Yet here each one of us is, surrounded by all the bright colors and the glittering promises.

All I have to do to be happy in the Land of I is to make the right choices among all the possibilities and opportunities that are flashing so insistently around me. What products will give me satisfaction, pleasure and status? What clothing will show me off to best advantage? What amusements will entertain? What friends will best fulfill my needs? What education will lead to the most satisfying career? What family will enhance my happiness? What choices will maximize my power and influence? What good works, even, can I undertake to fulfill my urge toward generosity and compassion?

If I choose well, I can have a good life and perhaps leave my mark on the world. If I stumble, I can correct and make a better selection. If I fall, I can get up and try again. If I continue to struggle, it must be because I have made too many bad choices.

In the Land of I, every person also gets a pair of rose-colored glasses—to make the colors and the promises more seductive, and to obscure the hard realities that nobody really wants to look at anyway. Immersed in the bustle and hype of the Land of I, it's hard to imagine any other world. Yet one is there and available to all of us, just a click of the heels away.

This world is quieter. The choices are less insistent. The lights flash less, but burn more steadily. Rose-colored glasses are nowhere to be found, and we see things happening to others around us that make us grieve. There are still individual choices, but they are more subtle. How is my life entwined with those around me at this moment—and the next—and what attitude can I hold, what step can I take, that will increase our overall welfare? In the longer term, how can I orient and equip myself to make my best and fullest contribution to this world, and how can I help others to do the same?

No longer in the Land of I, we don't have to make all these choices on our own. In this world, others don't care so much about the glitter of our clothes or social circles or careers, but they are deeply invested in promoting our gifts, our goodness and our potential.

None of us have to abandon our own center to live here; rather we all get to inhabit it more fully as each person finds a place in the middle of ever-greater circles of "we." We get to be for ourselves and for others at the same time. But first we have to make the decision to leave the Land of I. If we can take off those rose-colored glasses, turn our backs on the glitter and the empty promises and start claiming our connections, together we can find our way back home.

* * *

To find solutions to the economic mess we're in, we have to shift the whole conceptual frame from one of encouraging individual pursuit of private gain to one of valuing community. Luckily we have a deeper reality than nineteenth-century economic theory on our side here. Study after study confirms our spiritual belief that we human beings are hard-wired for connection and cooperation. Not only that, we simply don't exist as independent entities; the molecules of water that make up our body have been shared by countless other beings over billions of years—and we share 35% of our DNA with a daffodil! Somehow the way we work together to provide for our common welfare must better reflect the reality of this connection.

In our personal lives

While there is much we can do individually to cultivate attitudes and habits that align with what is needed for a new economy, there is no way we can find our way into a new reality alone. Community, that powerful antidote to both individualism and separation, is a necessity. But functioning in community is a process that requires intention and skill.

Even in groups where we have much in common, there are traps and snares. An assumption that we are all alike can be problematic in itself, blinding us to the many ways in which our experiences differ. Blind spots seem especially common around economic means and assumptions about the money we have or don't have. Challenges can range from attitudes of entitlement and unawareness around class and race, to being tightfisted and losing opportunities to spend on things of real value, to an attitude of judgment that seems always to lead to separation.

Many forces in society push us toward separation. Not only is individualism rampant, but oppression—of race, class, ethnicity, religion—is real, and the divisions it creates are hard to overcome. Voices in the media and politics grow ever more skillful at setting us apart and pitting us against each other.

Yet, whenever we feel better than, not as good as, fundamentally different from, without access to, unwelcomed by, or disinterested in any other group, there is the taint of separation which will keep us from the world we want.

How can we challenge this separation? I remember struggling to come to terms with a story I read in the newspaper about a woman of my age who lived not far from me. One of her sons was in jail for murder, another had just been killed, and she had to pick up the pieces and raise her grandchildren. How could I, in all my privilege, relate to this woman, my neighbor? Yet, if I can expand my reality, we have much in common. We both live in the midst of enormous injustice and hardship, we have both woken up alive this morning, we are both survivors in a tattered world, we both have this day to do our best.

A wise friend once suggested that, if in the course of our daily lives we aren't crossing paths with people from whom we've been separated by race or class, then we need to change the course of our daily lives. This involves awkwardness and making visible mistakes of commission (rather than the more hidden and comfortable ones of omission). It involves learning hard things—about the world and about ourselves—that we would rather not face. But the prize is getting each other.

As we are able to find more connection and common ground with people and groups from whom we have been separated, not only will our ability to create new possibilities and to challenge existing structures be strengthened, but a new vision of what security looks like may begin to take clearer shape.

Reflection: Rethinking security

A few years ago, I had the opportunity through work to meet a lovely family who run an early childhood program in a poor part of the city not far from where I live. I liked them a lot and was glad they wanted some of the tomato seedlings I had brought to the meeting to share. We talked about the garden they were hoping to start that spring, and I dropped some kale and collard seedlings off at their center.

I arranged to have them host one of our meetings the following spring. We had another long gardening conversation, and they showed us the raised beds they had built in a big empty lot down the street. Seeing that expanse of space, I spent time over the next several weeks separating perennials in our community garden and starting a little nursery to share.

Then one Saturday, I worked with them for three hours, hauling dirt, planting vegetables in the sunny back, and putting the flowers out front where they could be enjoyed by passersby. I came home with new friends, and a jar of their homemade barbeque sauce. They got a jar of my currant juice and a recipe for currant sorbet in return. I'd love to see if we can get some hardy perennials to take hold in the vast rocky middle of that lot. Mostly I'm looking forward to being friends.

This experience has mostly just given me pleasure, but it can also be seen as an investment in my long-term security. This is not money in the bank in the traditional sense and won't by itself support me in my old age. But it has real value nonetheless. Putting time into building these human assets may make as much sense as working extra hours to save for an individual future. In a neighborhood that was easy to think of as other, I now feel a deep point of connection. My extended family has grown and my world is safer.

* * *

I feel safer when I connect with my neighbors. I feel safer when I share with people far away, through such groups at the Quaker Right Sharing of World Resources with their wonderful mission of *relieving the burdens of both poverty and materialism.* The conclusion is inescapable: my security requires connection.

In our wider communities

Community-based projects can both support the local economy and provide a locus of innovation that can be replicated elsewhere. The Transition Movement, a campaign to build local resilience in the face of the threat of peak oil, is bursting with such innovations. Locally-sourced businesses, coops, farmers markets, community solar projects, and time banks, to name just a few, are springing up everywhere—a very hopeful antidote to the withdrawal of resources from community that comes with financial speculation and global corporate control.

There are community-based ways of managing money as well. Our Quaker yearly meeting, whose paradoxical dependence on the stock market for our financial health sparked that group head-scratching, is a case in point. As some of us were pondering how to get leverage to shift that bureaucracy off of dead center, a newcomer to the process found a way that the principle from one of the many funds in our endowment could be invested directly and locally in promoting the mission of that fund. With this wedge, we are more strongly situated to crack open a longstanding institutional belief that the stock market is the only game in town.

Or we can build on the example of local credit unions, and consider the options for public banks at municipal and state levels. (The Bank of North Dakota, the only state bank in the US, has done much to keep local resources from being drained out to big national and international banks and financial markets, and helped the state ride out the national recession of 2008 with minimal economic dislocation.)

Community also supports the taking of courageous action against economic injustice and violence. We can learn from a vibrant little group in Philadelphia called Earth Quaker Action Team. After taking on a big local bank with old Quaker ties over their investment in mountaintop removal (and winning!) they now have their sights on the local electric utility, calling for massive investment in solar and local solar jobs. They've built a life-affirming community of activists whose goal is a power shift and who aren't afraid to directly challenge those who currently hold it.

Since our economic system depends on getting people to act individually and on the basis of greed, any efforts to retain parts of the economic system in community, or return them to community are part of the solution. Thus we need to be alert for ways to support efforts that encourage increased cooperation and sharing, that increase local democracy, and that protect our common assets.

We can support legislation that makes it easier for producer and consumer cooperatives to start up, get access to favorable financing, and compete with businesses that are oriented toward maximizing private shareholder returns. We can pay attention to policies that encourage land trusts. We can oppose privatization of municipally-managed services, and support municipal ownership. We can lend our weight to efforts that strengthen the infrastructure for locally-based renewable energy systems.

The idea of subsidiarity, that nothing should be done by a larger organization which can be done as well by a smaller one, can be applied to governance as well as production. Who knows better the strength, potential and needs of a particular place, and who has greater motivation to see it flourish than those who live there? Yet the trend in our "bigger is better" world has been in the opposite direction, with decision makers having less and less contact with those whom their decisions impact. While there is a place for national—and international—government, steps to devolve power and resources back to local entities could help support human scale, and human well-being, in our communities.

A wonderful book on the commons by Jay Walljasper is called *All That We Share*. There are threats to the commons on all sides: loss of rainforests and top soils, pollution of water and air, schemes to privatize information, seeds, the airwaves, even genomes. Any efforts to protect our common shared wealth for the benefit of all—our soil, our water and air, our cultures and knowledge—will enrich our communities.

Sometimes a simple effort to address a community need can grow into something much bigger. A school nurse in a small old mining town joined her local borough council mostly to challenge an "old boys" network, but she became increasingly concerned about plans for the dumping of toxic sludge and coal fly ash in abandoned mines on the edge of town. It was shocking to discover how little power her town had to protect its people from these faceless corporations. With some support from a community rights organization, she proposed a Community Bill of Rights for her borough. It said that they had a right to act to protect their community from external harm. That their human rights were inalienable and took precedence over property rights. That nature has rights too.

This Community Bill of Rights passed a borough council vote (narrowly), the toxic sludge and fly ash corporations were told to stay away, and the world had its first example of legislation declaring that nature has rights. Other municipalities were inspired to follow suit. Some folks in Ecuador, then in the process of rewriting their Constitution took notice, and there is now language there saying that nature has the right to "integral respect for its existence." The power of the caring we have for the well-being of our communities cannot be underestimated.

Conclusion

Be patterns, be examples in all countries, places, islands, nations, wherever you come, that your carriage and life may preach among all sorts of people, and to them; then you will come to walk cheerfully over the world, answering that of God in everyone, whereby in them ye may be a blessing, and make the witness of God in them to bless you.
George Fox, 1656

Faced with an economic system that lacks integrity, fosters inequality, promotes greed, encourages extraction, does violence to people and planet, and compromises community, we need to dig deep to gather the spiritual resources to respond. To speak powerfully to that of God in everyone, as George Fox advises, we need to cultivate an overall way of being, a state of mind and heart, that keeps us fully in the present, and in living relationship with the world around us. There are also specific muscles to develop—around our abilities to repair, grieve, hope and act with courage.

Claiming the present

I struggle at my little plot in the community garden with waiting too long to harvest my vegetables. I'm always waiting for them to grow just a little bit bigger, or saving them for when I might need them more. It's particularly hard in the spring, when everything edible that's made it through the winter seems like a miracle. You don't want to just gobble up your miracles! But if I wait too long, they get bitter or tough, or fall off the vine.

I'm not a big spender in general, while I'm a very good saver, so I guess this attitude toward the garden shouldn't surprise me. But it really doesn't make sense. As I promise myself this year to pick generously and go for the goal of using everything up, I find myself pondering the larger question of spending and saving. Are there other things that are better spent than saved?

Clearly, for starters, there is our time. One of the problems with all the emphasis in our culture on technology that helps us save time is that it offers no help in making wise decisions about spending it. Yet if we don't choose to spend our time today, it's gone.

When we think about energy, spending often has a negative connotation. We have expended too much, or it is spent. Conservation is seen as wise. True, it's not good to push our bodies beyond their capacity, or deny them rest when they have been assaulted and need to recover. But in a way, our energy is like our time. If we don't make choices about how to spend today's supply, it's gone forever.

Then there is caring. Again, the inclination to be protective and spend it cautiously is strong. We want to put our caring into safe investments, where we can count on it yielding good returns. This is understandable, given how often it has been abused, starting when we were very young. But from another perspective, it is our nature to care, and withholding today will not increase the amount we have for tomorrow. If we can get access to that well of natural caring, there is an endless supply (though we'll probably have to grieve as well, to keep the channels clear). We can care hugely, every day, and there will still be the same amount left. In an economy of caring, it always makes sense to spend.

Money may be the hardest. Good arguments can be made for both spending and saving. But I wonder, if we put our attention to being big spenders in other ways—in time and energy and caring—maybe the money choices will be easier to sort out.

In the meantime, I plan to harvest this season with more thought to the present, picking my vegetables when they are in their prime, putting my faith in the seeds and the land's ability to produce again.

Relational living

I have been puzzled over the years by how tenacious I get in mending torn and broken possessions. Sometimes it seems ridiculous. Why not, for goodness sake, just throw them out and get something that will work?

It has occurred to me that the issue is one of relationship and service. When I buy something new, it serves me. I am in the relationship of master or mistress to that possession. I have it at will. I have placed some value on the service it can provide me, and expect it to serve me well. If it ceases to play the role I expect of it, there is every reason to replace it with something that does.

Once I start repairing, however, there is a relational shift. Now that my time and skill have gone into making that thing whole again, the relationship is more one of peers. It serves me, and I serve it to the best of my repairing ability. Sometimes it doesn't do as well as I would wish, and sometimes my repairs are inadequate—and I am the one found wanting.

When I noticed that a seam was coming undone in my serviceable brown sweater, I took a few minutes to make a neat repair, glad for the skill that made the task so easy. Later it was more seams, a small hole in the back, and a missing button. This repair took a little more time, and more ingenuity. As I studied it for anything I might have missed, I felt a new sense of connection. This sweater had a new lease on life because of my care, and I cared for it more as a result.

As I mend more, I care more. The challenge then becomes when to acknowledge that something I have cared about has come to the end of its useful life, to find a way to dispose of it fittingly, and to mourn its loss. The acquisition of a replacement becomes bittersweet, and brings with it all the weight of a new relationship.

But I have no regrets. I would rather have all the responsibilities of a give and take relationship, where I sometimes do well and sometimes fall short, than be in the role of master, surrounded by servant/slave possessions that exist at my pleasure and are likely to be discarded at the first sign of frailty or imperfection. Sometimes, I have to admit, it can feel like I'm running a nursing home, and there is relief in letting one of them go. It can be lovely to have something new that works to perfection. But I'm still glad to have the skills to prolong so many good and useful lives. I would never want to give up that sense of connection, and all that opportunity to care.

Mending the world

Our world is torn and broken. Many parts of it are not working. There are great tears and gashes, holes and frayed edges. What it needs is mending. And in general that's something we're not very good at. Ours is a culture of disposability, producing things with an intentionally short life so that it can sell us more. But we can't throw out the world. It's been around for quite a while, and it's worth saving. Besides, it's the only one we have. So—we have to learn to mend.

Mending and repairing are homely skills, hardly at first glance the stuff of ushering in a new age. Yet our society is fascinated with and addicted to what is new. We've been deeply conditioned to discard the old and go for the latest in glitz, ease or convenience at the drop of a hat. This ends up encompassing not only products of all kinds, but activities, and relationships as well. We've been trained to abandon things that aren't working well, since something better appears to be right on the horizon.

Not only does this attitude do violence to our earth and our human connections, but it disrespects our abilities to make things right. A new age will require enormous attention to conservation, to making things last. Any time we can see the possibility that something of value can be repaired, we are affirming an attitude of care and respect for the world around us.

What if we thought of mending as a critical activity in our quest for a truly livable world? Then every time we sewed a button, or apologized, or glued a chair rather than throwing it out, we could remember that we are building the skills, muscles and attitudes that are needed to make our world whole.

Reclaiming the ability to grieve

To pierce the numbness that allows us to accede to evil, and to maintain our capacity to expect and hope, we must be able to grieve. If we don't have that capacity, then we have to protect ourselves from anything which might cause grief. We can't court joy, feel fully, invest in that which may be unattainable. To ward off any danger of lows, we must refrain from setting our sights high, protecting ourselves from disappointment by not expecting much.

Yet grief is such a natural part of living. I've learned to see the expression of grief as integral to the healing process. As a parent of small children, I could watch it happen before my eyes. My children wanted something and couldn't get it, or lost something they loved—and they cried. If I held them in my arms and loved them and just let them cry, after a while they would be done, and would go back to life with renewed enthusiasm, ready to want and love again.

Much that is wrong in our world can be traced to an inability to grieve. What are despair and vengeance but indicators of aborted grieving? Incessant, desperate protest may have similar roots. For our love to stay accessible, we need to be present to all that is wrong, love what could be, and find ways to be overwhelmed with open-hearted grief. I was helped by a group at our Quaker Meeting that gathered for Lamentation—to grieve together about the state of the world. The actual lament can take many forms—questions born of anger and pain, tears, prayers, calls for help. Being able to open our hearts to the pain, and cry out our despair like a child in a parent's loving arms, consistently left us more ready to embrace the world in all its joys and sorrows.

A discipline of hope

Exercising a discipline of hope is something quite different from enjoying the feeling of hope. It is a repeated decision to be present to the goodness of reality regardless of all the pressing reasons for despair. Yet despair, as some wise person pointed out, is an insult to the future, and, as I think about the critical shortages in our world today, hope for the future may be the most critical—and the one in shortest supply.

So those of us who are interested in ushering in a new era will need to ground ourselves in hope. This involves getting access to perspectives and information that are not readily available in the media. It means talking about things that give us hope. In my e-mail column/blog, "Living in this World," I have taken on the discipline of including some things that make me feel hopeful every month—and I hear of people who skip through the essay or poem to get to those hopeful things. I sometime have to wrack my brains, or do some research, but my goal is to have four things, spanning global, national, local, and just plain human if possible, that genuinely give me hope.

We need hope to imagine a new future. For many of us, it's easier to imagine the end of the world than a new economic system—and this is a lethal failure of the imagination. The world needs people who can exercise their imagination muscles, weave new realities from the most insubstantial of threads, be able to say "this is real" even when nobody else around can see it—and to act on that reality. We need to practice stepping with confidence and hope into the unknown.

Cultivating courage

These are times that call for enormous courage—to face down evils of a magnitude that has never been seen before, to face loss and privation, to welcome chaos, to reach for connection way beyond our comfort level.

British Quaker Rex Ambler suggests the need for a kind of

courage that challenges separation, turning away from anxious attempts to fix the world from the outside toward claiming our place in the midst of a remarkable creation which has lost its sense of itself. As we cherish the whole and our place within it, seeing both the potential and the brokenness in ourselves and our world—"minding the oneness" as early Quakers said—we become able to bear witness more powerfully.

It takes courage to look at hard realities, to love big, to imagine a new thing that is yet unseen, and to act together with all the power at our command. Yet how many of us are brave?

What if we each did a personal inventory of the times and places where we have been courageous, and brought them to our community for acknowledgment and celebration? Looking at where our fears keep us quiet and passive, we could share our intentions to practice being brave—in our families, at work, with our neighbors, in the larger community—and come back to share our successes, or grieve our failures, and get ready to back each other on the next courageous step.

* * *

We are enmeshed in a giant stumbling economic system that has lost its way, straying far from its divine vocation and causing immense harm. But we are not immobilized and we need not be silenced. The issues are way bigger than us, but nothing will shift if we don't act. After all, we are God's hands.

We have many roles: in our families, as debtors, investors, community members, workers, citizens. There are many steps we can take from where we are standing right now to align our lives more closely with these Quaker testimonies, in our households, with our neighbors, congregations and wider communities, and through adding our weight to social movements and shifts in public priorities.

When folks in the US were urged by our president to respond

to the attacks on the World Trade towers by shopping, I asked my father, now an aging economist, for his perspective. I knew this wasn't the path that would guide us safely into the future. But what was? He said that the search is not for a different economic theory that works better, but for a theory of life that goes beyond economics as we currently know it.

There are so many unknowns about the future. The energy we spend second-guessing or judging our choices or those of others is mostly wasted. We get to do the best we can, relying on the power of moving forward in faith. Together, we make the path by walking.

Resources

Quaker Institute for the Future, www.quakerinstitute.org
New Economics Foundation, www.neweconomics.org
The Next System, www.thenextsystem.org
New Economy Coalition, www.neweconomy.net

CHRISTIAN
ALTERNATIVE

THE NEW OPEN SPACES

Throughout the two thousand years of Christian tradition there
have been, and still are, groups and individuals that exist in
the margins and upon the edge of faith. But in Christianity's
contrapuntal history it has often been these outcasts and
pioneers that have forged contemporary orthodoxy out
of former radicalism as belief evolves to engage with and
encompass the ever-changing social and scientific realities. Real
faith lies not in the comfortable certainties of the Orthodox,
but somewhere in a half-glimpsed hinterland on the dirt track
to Emmaus, where the Death of God meets the Resurrection,
where the supernatural Christ meets the historical Jesus,
and where the revolution liberates both the oppressed and
the oppressors.

Welcome to Christian Alternative ... a space at the edge where
the light shines through.
If you have enjoyed this book, why not tell other readers by
posting a review on your preferred book site.

Recent bestsellers from Christian Alternative are:

Bread Not Stones

The Autobiography of An Eventful Life

Una Kroll

The spiritual autobiography of a truly remarkable woman
and a history of the struggle for ordination in the Church of
England.

Paperback: 978-1-78279-804-0 ebook: 978-1-78279-805-7

The Quaker Way

A Rediscovery

Rex Ambler

Although fairly well known, Quakerism is not well understood.
The purpose of this book is to explain how Quakerism works as
a spiritual practice.

Paperback: 978-1-78099-657-8 ebook: 978-1-78099-658-5

Blue Sky God

The Evolution of Science and Christianity

Don MacGregor

Quantum consciousness, morphic fields and blue-sky
thinking about God and Jesus the Christ.

Paperback: 978-1-84694-937-1 ebook: 978-1-84694-938-8

Celtic Wheel of the Year

Tess Ward

An original and inspiring selection of prayers combining
Christian and Celtic Pagan traditions, and interweaving their
calendars into a single pattern of prayer for every morning
and night of the year.

Paperback: 978-1-90504-795-6

Christian Atheist
Belonging without Believing
Brian Mountford
Christian Atheists don't believe in God but miss him: especially the transcendent beauty of his music, language, ethics, and community.
Paperback: 978-1-84694-439-0 ebook: 978-1-84694-929-6

Compassion Or Apocalypse?
A Comprehensible Guide to the Thoughts of René Girard
James Warren
How René Girard changes the way we think about God and the Bible, and its relevance for our apocalypse-threatened world.
Paperback: 978-1-78279-073-0 ebook: 978-1-78279-072-3

Diary Of A Gay Priest
The Tightrope Walker
Rev. Dr. Malcolm Johnson
Full of anecdotes and amusing stories, but the Church is still a dangerous place for a gay priest.
Paperback: 978-1-78279-002-0 ebook: 978-1-78099-999-9

Do You Need God?
Exploring Different Paths to Spirituality Even For Atheists
Rory J.Q. Barnes
An unbiased guide to the building blocks of spiritual belief.
Paperback: 978-1-78279-380-9 ebook: 978-1-78279-379-3

The Gay Gospels
Good News for Lesbian, Gay, Bisexual, and Transgendered People
Keith Sharpe
This book refutes the idea that the Bible is homophobic and makes visible the gay lives and validated homoerotic

experience to be found in it.
Paperback: 978-1-84694-548-9 ebook: 978-1-78099-063-7

The Illusion of "Truth"
The Real Jesus Behind the Grand Myth
Thomas Nehrer
Nehrer, uniquely aware of Reality's integrated flow, elucidates
Jesus' penetrating, often mystifying insights – exposing
widespread religious, scholarly and skeptical fallacy.
Paperback: 978-1-78279-548-3 ebook: 978-1-78279-551-3

Do We Need God to be Good?
An Anthropologist Considers the Evidence
C.R. Hallpike
What anthropology shows us about the delusions of New
Atheism and Humanism.
Paperback: 978-1-78535-217-1 ebook: 978-1-78535-218-8

Fingerprints of Fire, Footprints of Peace
A Spiritual Manifesto from a Jesus Perspective
Noel Moules
Christian spirituality with attitude. Fourteen provocative
pictures, from Radical Mystic to Messianic Anarchist, that
explore identity, destiny, values and activism.
Paperback: 978-1-84694-612-7 ebook: 978-1-78099-903-6

Readers of ebooks can buy or view any of these bestsellers by clicking on the live link in the title. Most titles are published in paperback and as an ebook. Paperbacks are available in traditional bookshops. Both print and ebook formats are available online.

Find more titles and sign up to our readers' newsletter at
http://www.johnhuntpublishing.com/christianity
Follow us on Facebook at
https://www.facebook.com/ChristianAlternative